THE BL
OF IL

By the same author:

BEHOLD HIS LOVE
FATHER OF COMFORT (Daily Readings)
FOR JERUSALEM'S SAKE I WILL NOT REST
IF I ONLY LOVE JESUS
IN OUR MIDST – JESUS LOVES AND SUFFERS TODAY
IT SHALL COME TO PASS
MY ALL FOR HIM
NEVER BEFORE IN THE HISTORY OF THE CHURCH
PRAYING OUR WAY THROUGH LIFE
REALITIES – The miracles of God experienced today
REPENTANCE – The joy-filled life
RULED BY THE SPIRIT
THOSE WHO LOVE HIM
WELL-SPRING OF JOY (Songs of the Sisters of Mary for praying or singing)
WHEN GOD CALLS – The personal story of M. Basilea Schlink
WORLD IN REVOLT
YOU WILL NEVER BE THE SAME

By the Sisters of Mary:

THIS IS OUR GOD

THE BLESSINGS OF ILLNESS

BASILEA SCHLINK

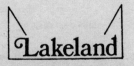

LAKELAND
116 BAKER STREET
LONDON W1M 2BB

First British Edition 1973

ISBN 0 551 00446 0

Unwin Brothers Limited
The Gresham Press, Old Woking, Surrey

Contents

"Why me?
Why has illness struck
          me down?"
"Because God wants you
to be near to Him –
          yes, you!"
When blessed with health,
          you came not near.
So many things to you
          were dear.
But now God calls to you
          in grace.
Come home to Him;
          'twill be too late
If you delay –
          death seals your fate.
Apart from God, eternity
Will only pain
          and heartache be.

God's Word brings strength to the sick and weak

Even though I walk through the valley of the shadow of death, I fear no evil; for Thou art with me; Thy rod and Thy staff, they comfort me.   Ps. 23: 4

He gives power to the faint, and to Him who has no might He increases strength.   Isa. 40: 29

Even youths shall faint and be weary, and young men shall fall exhausted; but they who wait for the Lord shall renew their strength, they shall mount up with wings like eagles, they shall run and not be weary, they shall walk and not faint.   Isa. 40: 30–31

But He said to me, "My grace is sufficient for you, for my power is made perfect in weakness."   2 Cor. 12: 9

It is good that one should wait quietly for the salvation of the Lord.   Lam. 3: 26

Behold, we call those happy who were steadfast. You have heard of the steadfastness of Job, and you have seen the purpose of the Lord, how the Lord is compassionate and merciful.   Jas. 5: 11

The paths of illness are God's ways of love

This little book for sick people is written out of my own experience, after many years of ill health. For I have suffered many illnesses. Some were not critical, yet they kept me in bed for months, preventing me from working. In fact it often seemed as though my work would come to a complete standstill. One, which lasted for several years, kept me awake with pain for hours every night. I felt so weak during the day that it was only with the greatest effort that I was able to continue my ministry. Later, I had a very severe illness, which brought me to death's door. I lay in hospital for many weeks, with my life in the balance. Day and night my body was racked with pain and my mind with questions.

It was during this time that I came to realise that, just as illnesses differ from one another, so our need for comfort varies with each illness. For each one we need a specific kind of comfort. Some illnesses burden our souls. Others bring much bodily pain and cause great inconvenience. But each has been chosen for us personally, by our Father, out of love for us. Jesus can transform every trial and trouble into blessing, if only we trust in His love; if only we accept His will and follow His way. The misery of illness will be changed into a blessing, according to God's plan, if only we will accept the suffering; if only we will rest in God's hands when He strikes us down.

But is not Jesus also our Physician as well as our Saviour? Will He not heal our infirmities? Has He not broken the power of sickness so that the one who believes on Him will receive healing—today, just as long ago? Certainly, Jesus came as Saviour and Healer of body, mind and spirit. Over and over again, people have experienced through faith and prayer, or through the laying on of hands, that the Lord has touched their body and made them well.

It is especially through His blood that we are offered His healing power. So, during those days of illness, it became very important to me to receive Communion. In this service He offers us His own body and blood. Yes, we can in faith expect that He will enter our sick body with resurrection power. Paul told the Corinthians that it was because they did not partake of Communion in the right manner, that there were so many sick and weak members in their congregation (1 Cor. 11: 30).

When illness strikes us, we must accept it with love and thanksgiving, as we would accept anything that the Father gives us. Then, with childlike trust, we shall be able to talk to our heavenly Physician about it. Just as we go to a doctor, so we should go to Jesus, telling Him all about our pain. We can ask for His help, with the sure knowledge that His blood has power to heal us. Always He is ready to help.

If we do this we shall sometimes experience His immediate healing. But because we are truly children of God, we may also experience that "the Lord disciplines him whom He loves" (Heb. 12: 6). Scripture tells us clearly that the Father must chasten His children. Sometimes He does not heal us, but allows us to drink a cup of suffering. But this is always in order that He may heal our souls, for eternity.

Our Lord Jesus is not only a Healer of our body; He is also a Healer of our soul, and to Him, our soul is more important than our body. Through our physical suffering, He is able to heal the soul. As the Bible says, "whoever has suffered in the flesh has ceased from sin" (1 Pet. 4: 1). If our illness has kept us from work, it will make us more dependent upon God. We must be still, and turn to Him in a different way from previously. So we learn to listen to God's voice. We begin to look at things in their right perspective and to see our life in His light. This brings us blessings which we would not have experienced if we had not fallen ill.

A period of prolonged suffering will show us how little patience we have, how demanding and touchy we really are. A time of sickness often results in situations which bring to light our weak and sinful points. Perhaps we feel that our relatives, friends or those who nurse us are not giving us the love and sympathy we want; they do not seem to understand, they apparently have so little compassion. This brings out all our touchiness, bitterness and selfishness. Thus it will teach us to pray for true humility and the selflessness which makes no demands upon others. Jesus works in us in order to transform us into His likeness.

God may strike us down with a serious disability, such as a damaged heart or lung, or deafness; or we may become a complete invalid, unable to continue our work or profession. If this happens, it brings special suffering. It makes us dependent upon others and we feel humiliated.

But this is the kind of illness that is specially able to make us humble. Also it teaches us to become dependent upon our heavenly Father and to cling to Him in faith. We learn to trust Him and to depend upon His help. Then we shall really discover how much He is mindful of those who suffer. His love showers them with blessings. It is written that suffering brings glory. Therefore we should rejoice in tribulation (Rom. 5: 3).

The Scriptures regard suffering as something precious. That does not mean that we are to seek or pray for illness. But if God brings illness upon us, it is very important that we recognise in the illness His aim for us. It is an aim of love—eternal salvation for our soul! Yes, we can know that our body also will finally be healed. When our soul has been healed, renewed and made beautiful, then we shall receive a magnificent resurrection body for eternity. So we should praise and thank Him for illness.

God is not interested only in our present welfare— our well-being during this short time on earth. No! He is an eternal God and is interested in our life in eternity. He is concerned that we shall become healthy and transformed in preparation for eternal life. He longs to be able to give us a resurrection body full of power and glory. When our earthly body becomes weak and we must suffer in the flesh, our soul becomes purified. This, more than almost anything else, will prepare our resurrection body.

The New Testament recounts many miracles of healing, and these reflect God's glory more and more. Not only did the man who was healed "leap and praise God", but, we read "all the people saw him walking and praising God" (Acts 3: 8, 9). Indeed people who were eye-witnesses of the working of the Spirit in healing turned to the Lord (Acts 9: 35).

It is the same today. People are challenged afresh by Jesus, the Great Physician, whenever there are healings. The presence of the living Christ, who said, "I am the resurrection and the life", can be felt. Healings, which are effected in the name of Jesus, reveal to people that He still imparts His blessings today. His strength is given not only to revive soul and spirit, but also to heal the bodies of sick people and to awaken them to new life.

When the Bible relates stories of miracle healings, it often speaks of faith. Jesus said to the blind man, "Receive your sight; your faith has made you well" (Luke 18: 42). From this, many people have drawn the conclusion that healing depends upon our faith, and have assumed that the reverse must also be true: if we are not healed, it must be because we have not enough faith. Yet it is important to notice that not all the heroes of faith were given miraculous deliverance from their suffering. In Hebrews 11 there are many accounts of the miraculous intervention of God. But others are included among these heroes of faith, who suffered and yet had no such deliverance (vv. 35–39). Although the Bible reports many miracles of healing, it also mentions other sick people who were not healed. Paul did not miraculously heal his helper Epaphroditus, who was near to death (Phil. 2: 25–30). He left Trophimus ill at Miletus (2 Tim. 4: 20). He recommended a natural remedy to Timothy for his stomach trouble (1 Tim. 5: 23), and he himself had to suffer his "thorn in the flesh" (2 Cor. 12: 7).

13

It is often said that it is impossible to pray in faith, unless we are certain that God will perform a miracle. This is manifestly not so, for Jesus—although He certainly had faith—prayed, "Father, all things are possible to thee; remove this cup from me; yet not what I will, but what thou wilt." He did not demand a miracle—a way out of suffering—but He was completely at one with the will of the Father, whatever suffering it might bring.

If we do not pray in this spirit of Jesus, "not my will, but thine be done", we are not at one with the will of the Father. What we call our strong faith may well be our strong self-will and rebellion. So it is not God's way for us to demand healing from Him, as though it were our right. If we have this attitude, and He does not say "Yes" to us, we are in great danger of falling into despair. We may blame ourselves for not having sufficient faith. Or we may blame those around us, declaring that it is their lack of faith that hinders God's blessing. This can make us bitter and resentful against God Himself.

Certainly, as children of the Father, we should make use of all His precious gifts and we should pray for healing, but always in a spirit of repentance, realising that we do not deserve His goodness—that we need to be disciplined and refined. Then we will be able to accept a "No", as David did when his child died. We will praise God and trust His love even in the midst of our suffering, because we know He has our ultimate good in view.

Why do we suffer illness? The Scriptures say that God is to be glorified through our suffering. He is glorified when He performs a miracle of healing in us. Then His name is praised. But He is glorified just as much, perhaps even more, when someone bears an illness with patience and love for Jesus, in complete surrender to the will of God.

Many sufferers have been a living testimony to others because, in spite of their pain, they were radiant with joy—the joy that comes from Jesus alone. God has sometimes received more honour through people who have borne their illness in this manner than He has through a miracle of healing. It is perhaps a greater miracle that through the power of Jesus a person can overcome his suffering and pain and reflect the love, humility and selflessness of our Lord.

From my own illnesses I can testify that I have known both experiences. I have been touched by the Lord and made well and I have also been ill and remained ill for a long time. In the first instance, He intervened and healed me. In the second instance, I experienced His help in a different way. He gave knowledge and talents to the doctors who became His instruments. The medicines they prescribed were created by God to bring health to the sick.

But the most important thing that I want to say is that there is a definite blessing in sickness. This book is written to testify to this truth. Sickness brings us blessing in a way that no other suffering can. I shall never regret the times of illness in my life. As a sinner, I needed them. They disciplined, cleansed and transformed me. Each time I have come through an illness, I have discovered that it has brought rich blessings to my life. This is not only true of my own illnesses; it has also happened with my spiritual daughters. Illness has brought them many difficulties, great pain and much suffering. This little book has been compiled from these experiences and from letters, words of comfort and verses which I wrote for my daughters during such times.

It came into being through sickness, and it seeks to bring to others the things that helped me through my own days of illness and the times when those near to me were sick. My most precious experience in all these times of illness has been this—God our Father has a special love for those of His children who are afflicted and poor. This includes those who are sick. He has prepared for them special blessings and gifts of love. He wants to pour out His goodness upon them in a special way. Over them He has spread His covenant of love. He wants to prepare them for eternity and lead them along the way to great glory.

The sick and
        suffering
are the favoured of God.
He shows them
        special love
and attention.

Be assured
that right now you are
        especially loved,
even if in the midst
        of your pain
you are not
        aware of it.

A prayer for patience

My God and Master,

Give me patience to suffer this long illness without protest or complaint. I cannot manage this by myself. I keep looking for the reason, and asking, "Why should I be the one who is struck down?" It torments me and my heart rises up in anger. That is why I am looking for help from You.

O Jesus, You went the way of suffering and pain. Yes, You suffered to the bitter end. I thank You for understanding me. I call upon Your name, Jesus, because that name has power to help. You went ahead of us on the path of pain that leads to glory. Along this way You were perfected and glorified.

Through my path of suffering, remake me into a new person in whom You can live. Then I shall bear the image of God, for which we were created. Let my illness bring me home to You, my God, so that in eternity I may not abide in hell, but in Your kingdom of eternal joy.

When I cannot pray at length, I will speak these short sentences:

Lord Jesus, I thank You, because Your life has shown me that the illness with which You have blessed me will transform my soul. I know that I am precious and dear to You. Come, Lord, live in me and make me new.　Amen.

* * *

Do not think it unimportant when the Lord chastens you through illness. But understand that He will do great

things in this way. He wants to transform you miracu-
lously into the likeness of Jesus—the image of love,
patience, humility and meekness. Is there anything
greater than this in all eternity?

What illness can teach you about God

It will teach you not to worry any more. You will learn to leave to the Father, in His love, to decide what is best for you, both today and tomorrow.

It will teach you to be dependent upon Jesus, who in illness is your only help. Only He can turn sickness into health.

It wants to teach you the mightiest prayer, which is highly honoured in heaven: "My Father, Thy will be done."

It will not let you go until you accept the cross, until you pledge yourself to it, until you have learned to say "Yes, Father", and so cannot fall into despair.

It wants to teach you to humble yourself beneath the hand of God, because you recognise that "I, a sinner, need this experience".

It wants to teach you patience. Those who are patient will receive a crown, because they have endured to the end.

It wants to teach you to be meek when you are grieved by torments and hardships, so that you bear them without protest and rebellion.

It wants to teach you not to yearn for comfort and love, but to depend only upon God and to be triumphant over your irritability.

It wants to teach you to believe, even when human help has come to an end, that God is the Master of your body.

It wants to teach you not to think of yourself, but to suffer with others, to give them love and so forget your own suffering.

It wants to teach you the song in the night which brings thanks to God in suffering, because He gives us glory through suffering.

It wants to teach you to thank Him for suffering, because it prepares you for glory and brings blessings and joy without end.

It wants to teach you to bring forth the fruit for which God often looks in vain among His children, the fruit which only comes from suffering.

*   *   *

*Why does God chasten only me—
when others, who are not better
than I, remain well?*

*Thank God that He has specially chosen you.
Your life would have come to nothing,
but now it is to become wholly new,
because God loves you so much.*

A prayer for the proper fruit from days of illness

My Father,

I thank You for giving us a special blessing for the inner man in times of illness, and for speaking to us in the quiet about the way we have been leading our lives. So I pray that You will open my eyes in these days of weakness. Let me see my life in Your light and recognise where I have made You and others sad, where I have sinned against You and my fellow men.

I thank You for giving me in this illness a time of grace, a time for repentance, so that I can turn from my old life, my old habits and ways.

Let me go forth from this sick bed as a new creature who has not suffered Your chastening in vain, but who has become cleansed and transformed into Your likeness, for eternity. Help me to live in such a way as to be a joy for You and my fellow men when You give me new life and health. Amen.

The mirror of conscience

If we confess our sins, He is faithful and just, and will forgive our sins and cleanse us from all unrighteousness (1 John 1:9).

Realise that God wants to speak to you during your illness about your past life. He wants to give you the opportunity to confess your sins before it is too late and you come to His judgment and eternal punishment. Be penitent and receive forgiveness. Take advantage of this opportunity. In this connection the following questions will help you*:

How did I live my life before God placed me on this sickbed?

1. Was I living without a personal relationship to God, without daily times for prayer and reading the Bible? If so, I was living like a heathen, with no room in my life for God, except perhaps for a few minutes.
2. Have I disregarded God's commandments? Have I trespassed against them or have I even lived my life in constant rebellion against His laws? If so, my sin against God and other people now stands between me and God; I am under God's judgment and His anger is kindled against me. I must realise this now during my illness, or as I perhaps lie facing death.

* See also *Mirror of Conscience* and *You Will Never Be the Same*, by M. Basilea Schlink.

Have I taken to heart the sixth commandment? Or am I angry or offended by someone, perhaps a member of my family or someone with whom I work? Is there bitterness or anger in my heart, or an unwillingness to be reconciled?

Have I kept holy the eighth and ninth commandments, or have I taken something away from someone else? Perhaps from his honour, by gossiping or by putting him in a bad light?

Have I kept the seventh commandment and not sought any person of the opposite sex other than my spouse? Not even in my thoughts, or by giving him my love? Have I given way in the smallest respect to such a desire, and thereby practised adultery?

3. Who was my God? Whom was I ready to serve, to love, to give my interest and time? For whom did I make a sacrifice? Was it for people, my family, my job, my possessions or something else?

Were these my idols? If so, I was practising idolatry and thereby incurring God's anger. He is my Creator and Saviour; therefore He has a right to my love.

4. What kind of seeds have I sown during my life? Were they seeds of trust and love of God? Have I obeyed His commandments? Have I showed love and mercy towards all people, forgiving them? Have I done good to others, bringing them gifts and joy? If so, I shall harvest love and mercy. If I have sown hate, anger, mercilessness, strife, jealousy and greed, then I shall harvest anger and mercilessness when I come before God's judgment.

5. Has every guilt in my life been cleansed? That is, have I confessed my sins to a spiritual counsellor and asked and received forgiveness from Jesus? Have I confessed my sins to the people against whom I have sinned, and have I made amends to the best of my ability?

"For whoever has suffered in the flesh has ceased from sin." (1 Pet. 4: 1)

Consequently, through bodily suffering we have the opportunity to suffer away our sin and be purified. Take advantage of this opportunity.

God's Word reveals the hidden
blessings of illness

We know that in everything God works for good with those who love Him.   Rom. 8: 28

For the Lord disciplines him whom He loves, and chastises every son whom He receives.   Heb. 12: 6

For the moment all discipline seems painful rather than pleasant; later it yields the peaceful fruit of righteousness to those who have been trained by it. Heb. 12: 11

Behold, I have refined you, but not like silver; I have tried you in the furnace of affliction.   Isa. 48: 10

I consider that the sufferings of this present time are not worth comparing with the glory that is to be revealed to us.   Rom. 8: 18

So we do not lose heart. Though our outer nature is wasting away, our inner nature is being renewed every day.   2 Cor. 4: 16

For this slight momentary affliction is preparing for us an eternal weight of glory beyond all comparison, because we look not to the things that are seen but to the things that are unseen; for the things that are unseen are eternal.   2 Cor. 4: 17–18

Afterwards!

O Lord, my God, will this illness never end? One week follows another and I can see no ray of hope. There is no end in sight. I am told again and again, "Suffer in patience." However, God does not ask for our patience without giving it to us Himself. So He helped me in the following manner:

A visitor brought me a little card with a verse of which one word spoke to my heart like a bright star— AFTERWARDS! It came from the Word of God, and reads:

> Now no chastening for the present seemeth to be joyous, but grievous: nevertheless afterward it yieldeth the peaceable fruit of righteousness unto them which are exercised thereby.   Heb. 12: 11 A.V.

AFTERWARDS! This means that, after this illness, I can expect something very special, something I can look forward to as a child looks forward to Christmas.

I shall be permitted to pick a fruit which is very precious and wonderful to the taste. It is called the fruit of righteousness. This means that during this illness a part of me will be transformed, so that the heavenly Father can say to me, "Good! Now you are beautiful and pleasing to Me." Suffering is the crucible in which I shall be purified. Yes, through suffering the Lord Jesus imprints upon our hearts and souls His image of love, mercy, humility and meekness. He wants to do it now. Then we shall bear His image for eternity. All the humble and meek have been promised salvation. How happy I shall be above! "Suffering! Who can measure your worth? Here you are called a burden, but above you are called a blessing. You are a privilege which is not given to everyone."

A little word which brings bliss: AFTERWARDS! I experience a great happiness within me, looking forward to all that this AFTERWARDS will bring.

The father's way
is always good,
and even if it should
hurt you,
it will serve
for your healing.

The one who is precious
and truly of worth,
is tested through trouble
and sorrow —
only in this way
will you arrive
at the heavenly goal.

Illness is not without meaning

You complain:

"I have been put out of commission for a long time, lying in hospital, far away from friends and relatives. I am sick, and even if I do not want to admit it, death is standing at my door. My spirit seems to be climbing walls, for I want to live and work, and yet I seem to be almost dead. I am tormented by boredom; I can scarcely kill the time. I hunger for pleasure and joy, but my soul finds none!"

Listen to God's answer:

"Why have you been put out of commission? This illness did not come upon you without reason. No, it was sent to you, ordered especially for you, by your Lord and God. It is His hand that has laid this burden upon you. His wisdom thought of this path for you. He loves you, personally, and yearns so much for your love. He is seeking you and wants to draw you to Himself. That is why He brought you here where you are alone and lonely. Here your soul will seek the living God. Without Him you will never find peace, or true, lasting happiness. So come to Him, and do not try to escape from your boredom by seeking diversion, pleasure and variety.

No, begin to pray and seek for Him. Here on this sickbed your heart will find real life, which will fill you with lasting joy that no one can take away. You will find Jesus. He is life. He is joy. He is love. So give Him your life. Then one thing is absolutely sure: He will help you."

Dialogue between the sick soul and God

I cannot go on!
I have strength enough to carry you through.

My heart weeps!
I have comfort for you, the comfort of My love.

I cry: Why must I suffer?
I say to you: Those whom I love I will draw to My heart through suffering and illness, and give them new life.

I complain: What did I do to deserve such suffering?
I say to you: Know yourself before it is too late! You are filled with sin. That is why My chastening is but pure grace.

I complain: There is no one who really cares for me and loves me.
I say to you: Forget yourself and your needs. Give love and understanding to others, and you will see how much better off you are than they. You will see how much you are loved by Me.

Pain torments me greatly!
I will remind you of your Saviour—just picture His pain!

Fear of death torments me.
I say to you: "It is finished!" Death has been conquered! No one can tear you out of Jesus' hands.

I complain: I am so ill, completely helpless and dependent upon others.
I say to you: You are dependent only upon Me. I am sufficient for you; believe Me—I can bring joy to your heart. I will send to you people who will help you.

Worries torment me without ceasing.

I care for those who cannot care for themselves. I care for the sick and miserable. I will care for your family.

Is there any sense in this illness?

It is the hand of Jesus that leads you. The hand that was pierced for you on the cross. The hand that has done everything for you. You can truly believe that He will lead you to your goal if you yield to the will of God. His hand brings great blessings. It will create a new you— yes, a new you for eternity.

I am in despair. I cannot endure the fact that this illness has no end.

Keep your eyes on Jesus, who has always been patient. Ask Him for a gift, the gift of patience. The person who asks something of Jesus always receives. He will fill you with patience to suffer the burden of your illness.

I cannot pray; I cannot believe any more.

Let your heart just speak the name of Jesus. Tell Him everything that you lack, every need. Truly, if you pray even so simply, and believe, you will receive help.

I cannot work any more; I can no longer do anything creative.

Now you will learn that, by bearing suffering in the right way, you are doing something great that will last for ever more.

I am all alone, and I am not allowed to do anything.

Rest quietly in My arms and speak with Me. Yes, listen to My voice alone. Now I shall visit you, I who have always loved you and who have sought you anew through your illness.

My melancholy will crush me.

It cannot crush you, if you will humble yourself beneath

My hand. God will always exalt the humble—He quickens those who admit their guilt and who wait upon Him for help.

My thoughts plague me. I complain against my fellow men; my thoughts rebel against God and what He has done to me.

You have forgotten to turn your complaints against yourself. You have forgotten what you are doing to God when you make life difficult for others. Be thankful that I do not chasten you more. Give thanks for all the good things that you have, and your need will disappear.

I have resigned myself and am completely discouraged; I shall be an invalid all my life and shall be sickly and wretched.

I have put a thorn in your flesh so that you may become bound to Me, so that you cannot do anything without Me. You must live for Me alone. I gave you this thorn so that you may learn humility—your old self will be crucified. You will learn not to be bitter and touchy. In your weakness and poverty My strength, My blessing, My life will shine forth. Look to Me alone for love and help, and not to men. Then there will flow out from you a river of blessing without limit and without end.

Not alone!

I was separated from my loved ones for a long time because of my illness. Even while I was at home, I seldom saw them, because the doctor had ordered complete rest and few visitors. When I was taken to the hospital, I lay for several months almost completely alone.

But now I will tell you a secret! I was not really alone. One day a sister brought me a crucifix and hung it on the wall opposite my bed. It was a great help to me to gaze at the face of our Lord filled with agony. He who is love, suffered immeasurable pain beneath His crown of thorns, because He loves me.

So I was strengthened, and my faith renewed—He is with me! He loves me more than anyone else ever could. He has suffered and wept for me far more than anyone else has. Today He still suffers with me, for He is the living Lord. I can talk to Him at any time, and can tell Him what is in my heart. Yes, I can bring Him all my needs and the questions that trouble me. He understands them and answers them better than any man.

I was allowed to look at Him who bears God's image: Jesus. He is entirely merciful and humble. He is peace. As I looked at Him I experienced the truth of the words, "Look to Him, and be radiant; so your faces shall never be ashamed" (Ps. 34: 5). A profound peace entered my heart, and I was deeply comforted.

But that was not all. As I gazed at my crucified Lord and absorbed the essence of Jesus, I became able to trust that during my suffering I would become transformed. What we look upon continually, that we shall become. The Lord blessed me and I was able to yield completely to His will and to speak His words: "Yes, Father, Thy will be done!" So the misery of my illness was changed into blessing, peace and joy in Him.

Heal me, O Lord, and I shall be healed; save me, and I shall be saved; for thou art my praise.   Jer. 17: 14

And whatever you ask in prayer, you will receive, if you have faith.   Mt. 21: 22

Why are you cast down, O my soul, and why are you disquieted within me? Hope in God; for I shall again praise Him, my help and my God.   Ps. 42: 11

I sought the Lord, and He answered me, and delivered me from all my fears.   Ps. 34: 4

And will not God vindicate His elect, who cry to Him day and night? Will He delay long over them? I tell you, He will vindicate them speedily.   Lk. 18: 7–8

Therefore confess your sins to one another, and pray for one another, that you may be healed. The prayer of a righteous man has great power in its effects.   Jas. 5: 16

> *I call upon Your name.*
> *You are the Lord who can help.*
> *The power of every illness*
> *is subject to the risen Lord.*

A prayer before an operation

My Father,

You are my refuge, You alone. I call upon You, Lord, to bring me safely through this operation and to give me healing and help.

Guide the hand of the surgeon so that the operation is a success. I thank You, because I know that doctors are Your instruments and helpers. Nothing can happen to me except what You, my Father, in Your love have decided for me.

So take me in Your arms now, during the next few hours and for the following days. Then I can rest in You completely, **even** when I am unconscious. Let me behave throughout the operation in such a way that I do not bring disgrace to Your name. If by Your grace I wake up after the operation, then my first thought and my first words will be in thanks to You.

As I commit my whole being and life to You for this operation, let my whole life now come into Your light. I do not want to go into this operation without confessing all my sins to You, and where necessary to others also. I want to receive Your forgiveness.

My Lord Jesus, I await all that is coming to me, with the comforting knowledge that I am Yours and You are mine. Nothing can separate me from Your love either in life or death.   Amen.

A prayer after an accident

My Lord and God,

   You have used this accident to give me a frightening but beneficial experience. You have suddenly taken me out of my previous way of life. You have also reminded me that it is possible to be taken from this life and earth in a single moment to stand before Your throne of judgment.

   You permitted this accident in order to give me a loud trumpet call to wake up. You are warning me to live my daily life facing the fact of eternity. Yet through Your fatherly goodness, You have watched over me and saved me from death. I thank You for this.

   I know that not even a single hair of our head falls without Your will. You want what has happened to serve only for my best. Please let me recognize where my guilt lies and why this had to happen.

   Forgive me for the times when I have let myself be caught up in the mad rush of life, when I have not acted responsibly by keeping the traffic regulations, when I have endangered the lives of others or when I have brought damage or even injury to others. If in this particular accident the other person was more guilty than I, please keep me from all accusations and bitterness. Help me to forgive him from the bottom of my heart, because I daily experience Your forgiveness.

   I thank You, not only for having given me my life again, but also for letting me come to You and bring You all the sin and guilt which burden my soul. You will give me repentance. As I more and more comprehend Your forgiveness, I shall live more responsibly. I pray with all my heart that, if You heal me, You will help me to so order my life in the future, that I need not fear sudden death.

I bring You my family, my colleagues at work and others. Show me where I have broken Your commandments in relationship to each one. I will humble myself before all those against whom I have sinned.

You have made me into a new person. I intend to turn my back on my old life. I bring You this new life that You have given me. It shall be Yours, my Lord and Saviour. From now on I will follow You and obey Your commandments.   Amen.

A prayer trusting in the Father's help

My Father,

As Your sick child I ask You, "Please help me. I cannot go on bearing such suffering. Who else can help me but You, my Father? You have created me. You know my physical needs and You alone have the power to turn the course of my illness."

I bring my needs before You and pray: If it is Your will, please intervene in this situation. Help me to get well, so that I can serve You in my family. You gave me to them and they are waiting. But if You have decided differently, I will say, "Your will be done—Your will is best!" I will be a true child and humble myself beneath Your chastening hand. Then my burden will become light, because I will be receiving it from my Father's hand.

In spirit I shall kiss Your hand, my Father, and say, "Yea, Father, yea, most willingly, I'll bear what Thou commandest!" I know that You are looking upon me with love—as it is written: "The Lord disciplines him whom he loves" (Heb. 12: 6).

You are leading me through this illness for my eternal well-being. You will make me holy for eternity. Through the suffering of this illness You will prepare me to come to You for ever. So I place all my wishes and longings in Your hands. Do with me as You will. Let my illness last as long as You will. I know that You will do a perfect work.   Amen.

*   *   *

Place all your hope in the living God alone. Even doctors and medicines are subject to Him. They are His instruments. Realise that any day one single word from His lips can change your illness into health. Place your trust in God alone, the Almighty God of heaven and earth. He has all power over your illness.

*   *   *

As a sick person, never forget that Jesus is your Physician and Saviour. His blood has saving power. He can heal the ailments of our bodies. Call upon the healing name of the Saviour.

Holy Communion—an offer of grace to those who are sick

Come to me, all who labour and are heavy-laden, and I will give you rest. Mt. 11: 28

O taste and see that the Lord is good! Happy is the man who takes refuge in Him! Ps. 34: 8

The Lord Jesus calls us to Himself—He who is the Saviour of our bodies and our souls. Yes, there is in the Holy Communion power for body and soul; a creative, renewing power that changes and strengthens our bodies.

How often we turn to people for help when we are sick—whether it be in body, mind or spirit. We try all sorts of things, and spend a great deal of money, time and energy. Yet how often we completely forget our Lord's royal invitation: "Let him who is thirsty come, let him who desires take the water of life without price" (Rev. 22: 17). This is an offer to us from Jesus, a true offering. It is so clear, it cannot be mistaken. Yes! and it is free! He gave Himself in order that He could offer us this water of life. All others who invite us to a meal offer us something from their goods and possessions. All other helpers have a method of some sort, which they offer to strengthen and revive us. But the Lord who invites us to the Holy Communion gives Himself to be our food and drink. The Saviour Himself is the remedy. The secret of Holy Communion, the source of its power, is that the divine Being actually enters into us—the divine Being who is Love. How foolish we are, if we do not come to Him, especially when we are weak, sick or needy, to take in faith this rich gift of love which He offers us.

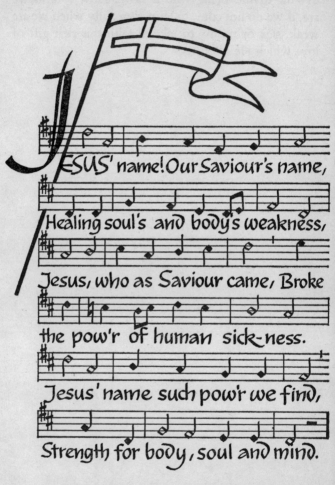

JESUS' name! Our Saviour's name,

Healing soul's and body's weakness,

Jesus, who as Saviour came, Broke

the pow'r of human sick-ness.

Jesus' name such pow'r we find,

Strength for body, soul and mind.

Well-spring of Joy 134

44

God's Word brings help to the sick

I am the Lord, your healer.   Exod. 15: 26

Behold, I will bring to it health and healing, and I will heal them and reveal to them abundance of prosperity and security.   Jer. 33: 6

Your hurt is incurable, and your wound is grievous. I will restore health to you, and your wounds I will heal.   Jer. 30: 12, 17

I have seen his ways, but I will heal him; I will lead him and requite him with comfort, creating for his mourners the fruit of the lips.   Isa. 57: 18

It was neither herb nor poultice that cured them, but thy all-healing word, O Lord.   Wisdom 16: 12 (N.E.B.)

He sent forth His word, and healed them, and delivered them from destruction.   Ps. 107: 20

He will deliver you from six troubles; in seven there shall no evil touch you.   Job 5: 19

Surely He has borne our griefs and carried our sorrows; upon Him was the chastisement that made us whole, and with His stripes we are healed.   Isa. 53: 4–5

BELIEVE—

BELIEVE
IN THE VICTORY
OF JESUS.

ILLNESS LIES
AT THE FEET
OF HIM

WHO IS RISEN!

Overcoming the special temptations of ill health

Do you know what it is that makes you so unhappy during your illness? What is it that makes it almost unbearable—that tortures you so much, you cannot cope with the misery? It is self-pity and ingratitude. You revolve around yourself and your illness. He who is freed from these sins will be at peace and able to bear his illness with courage. There are people in whom this can be seen. So this is the remedy: get rid of self-pity and all your concern about your illness; then it will no longer be able to make you unhappy, discouraged and despairing.

You ask, "How can I possibly get rid of self-pity and concern for myself?"

You must declare, "Before God and hell, I say No! to all my fear of suffering, to all thoughts of myself and of my illness and to all my worry. Therefore I renounce all self-pity, which only increases my pain. I renounce the spirit of despair and all the evil thoughts in my heart. I will no longer stare into the darkness.

"Further, I shall refrain from asking for love, care and visits, if these are selfish or inconsiderate demands. I say No! to my claims that everybody and everything possible be set into motion just to bring me mitigation and comfort. I shall reject every thankless and accusing thought against those upon whom I am dependent, who care for me and nurse me.

"I will not foster the smallest distrust of God's love. His love has led me into this illness, in order to give me special blessings. I will have nothing further to do with

47

such thoughts, because I belong to You, Jesus. I will go with You, the Man of Sorrows, along the way of the cross. I will follow You, trusting in Your love. You always have help ready for me, so I will say Yes! to my cross.

"I shall stand beneath Your cross, the symbol of victory. Before it the sinful power of my ego and its demands, my fear of pain, my impatience, my protests all have to yield. Yes, in Your name, Jesus, I surrender all these dark, worried, accusing thoughts. I shall counter each one with my thanks for all the good things which You have given me in my illness. I will also thankfully recall all the help which I have received from people."

(At this point it would be good to name all the things you are thankful for.)

"O Jesus, You have redeemed me and so You will make me into a thankful, unassuming, patient and loving person. I shall look to You, and then all bad thoughts will be cast into the abyss. Hallelujah!"

A request for strength to bear suffering

Dear Lord Jesus,

Give me the strength which I now need, the strength to endure suffering. I open my sad heart to You so that You can fill me with Your love. I surrender myself to follow in Your footsteps along the way of the cross—the way You are now leading me.

I open my mouth wide, so that You can fill it with words of deep gratitude for all the good which I am receiving through my illness. Fill it also with words of trust in Your love; You will never give me more than I can bear. Your love has measured and chosen this cross especially for me.

My Father,

I trust You and Your love. I trust Your power to help me, because it is far greater than all my needs in this illness.

Your love will therefore triumph over my illness. If I am unable to pray or to speak much, then I shall repeat in my heart this one sentence: "My Father, I trust You."

Your love always sends help to me, Your weak child. My Father, You love me, You will carry me through in Your strong arms. I rest trustingly and quietly in Your heart—I am Your child, my Father, and You feel such fatherly love for me. Yes, You are my Father! Amen.

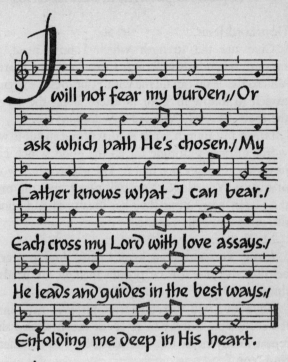

I will not fear my burden, Or
ask which path He's chosen. My
Father knows what I can bear.
Each cross my Lord with love assays.
He leads and guides in the best ways,
Enfolding me deep in His heart.

I follow Him with pleasure.
His care is past all measure,
He chooses all that's best for me.
When all is dark around me,
His loving arms surround me,
And He can deal
        with all my needs.

On being active in inactivity

On the table next to my bed there stands a picture:
Jesus with His hands bound tightly together. A kind
visitor brought me this picture to comfort me. She
knew how hard it was for me to lie there month
after month, unable to do anything. This visitor could
sense how I felt—as though my hands too had been
bound.

Yes, it seemed to me that one day Jesus, our mighty
Lord who has power to bind and to release, came and
bound me, so that I could no longer work and be
active. But He never left me alone. He came to me in
this picture and told me: "I am your Companion on
this path which you must travel. Look at My hands,
how tightly they are bound together—these hands
which did only good. They healed innumerable
people and helped them. They blessed them and
released them from all evil. They did many good
things. Yet the heavenly Father brought these hands
to rest. Now they are resting in My suffering; I became
a prisoner according to the eternal decree of the Father.

"But look at My picture again. It is My bound hands
which have achieved the greatest things for all people.
It was not My work and activity that brought them
deliverance. It was suffering and patience, My being
bound. Do you know anything of the strength that is
inherent in patience? It is the greatest strength of all.
It was through this strength that I brought salvation to
the whole world. Be willing to have your hands bound
to suffer and to endure pain. Be patient in your suffering, giving your will to God. Then great and eternal

things will be achieved through you too. A stream of blessing will flow out from you, imperceptibly, to many people. Also, while you are lying still, you will draw closer to Me—the One who loves you and is waiting for you."

Jesus, the Man of Sorrows, belongs to the sick and to those who are full of pain and sorrow. If they accept Him into their hearts and thank Him for His sufferings, they will receive strength to bear their own suffering.

A prayer for difficult nights

My Lord Jesus,

You see these nights full of agony, and You will help me to bear the pain. Let me suffer with You, O great Man of Sorrows. You can help me to bear it patiently, so that it will not seem so heavy. I thank You, Jesus, that in all Your pain, You were tempted just as I am. Therefore, You can now help me and I know You will. You will never let me be tempted beyond my strength. Yes, I thank You for giving us an example. You taught and proved that pain brings glory.

So I believe that great things will come from Your hand, if I accept my illness with humility—if I bear it with You and in love for You.

Yes, from each long and pain-filled hour of the night, a seed from my "Yes, Father" will germinate and produce fruit. And some day You will transform them into eternal glory and joy. So I will say, in each difficult hour: I will not notice the pain, distress and suffering, because through You such things will bring me glory. Amen.

A surrender to suffering

My Lord Jesus,

I come to You in utter weakness but with complete trust in Your strength. I give my "Yes" to every step You lead me during my illness. These steps rise up before me like mountains of cares. Nevertheless I give myself to You, Jesus, with an unconditional "Yes" to this cross of illness. No matter how hard it seems to me and no matter what may come, I will accept it.

I give myself to You, Jesus, the Man of Sorrows, in love for You. I will take up my cross of illness anew. I will follow You along Your road of the cross, in order to be an example to others and show them how You help Your followers to carry their crosses in patience and surrender to You.

I give myself to You, O Jesus. Even if my illness is not taken from me, I will not complain; I will carry my cross to the end in patience, and continue to repeat, "Yes, Father".

I give myself to You, my Jesus, and I will humbly allow others to help me, as You did. I will not demand help, but I will be thankful for all the care, treatment and medical advice which You send.

I say to You, my Lord Jesus: Let happen what You will, here I am. Do as You will with me during this illness. My father, You love me and You know what Your child needs. You are leading me in the best way. Therefore I commit myself completely to You and Your will.   Amen.

Just now you are not able to work, because the time has come for you to suffer. Suffer humbly before God, with a "Yes, Father". Give yourself completely to His chastening; trust that His love will sustain you. Then your suffering will bear more fruit than your working, because your ego will die, as a grain of wheat dies in the earth. And such dying brings forth real fruit.

* * *

you

will bear
my suffering with me.
Yes, You want
to prepare my heart
for the greatest
eternal blessing.
You know how short is
this earthly life,
therefore You are
giving me that
which will ultimately
bring
the greatest joy.

Four long months have gone by since I was taken ill. It is summer now, and visitors tell me how beautiful it is outside. They are deeply sorry for me, because I cannot see all this beauty or share in it. Yes, it is true, this year I must do without all this. I am like a small bird imprisoned in a cage, shut in behind four walls.

However, I am like a happily engaged girl. She loves the beauty of this world, but since she has come to love her fiancé so deeply, she is hardly aware of her surroundings. She only knows that he is with her and this is her joy. Sometimes he goes away for a while but he tells her to stay at home and wait for him. This she does gladly, because she knows that he will still be in her heart. Lovingly she accepts his wish that she should remain at home. She does everything he wishes, because he is her beloved.

I am like that happy bride-to-be. Jesus is my Friend, who loves me more deeply than any earthly bridegroom could. He is worthy of my ardent love. I love Him above everything, with all my strength and with my whole being. I also love His will which says, "Stay in this room. Lie here until I lead you elsewhere. I am with you." I could accept His will and His leading with love, although it meant a cross. I could accept it as a greeting from the One who loves me so much that He gave His life for me.

Yes, I am happy in my imprisonment because it binds me more deeply and more tightly to Him, my Jesus. It is the answer to my prayers of the last few years, "Nearer, my God, to Thee, nearer to Thee".

So I have been permitted to learn in my "prison" room that "Whoever has You is satisfied and at peace. He who depends on You needs nothing else." He came in order to give us a full life—abundant life. This I have learned during these past months. His love can make our happiness complete, so that we need nothing but Him.

Remain Steadfast in Obedience to God!

But how?

Out of Love for Jesus.

This will bring you a crown of glory.

An answer of love for Jesus whose love has sought us in illness

My dear Lord Jesus,

Through my illness You have led me into a great quiet. You drew me away from all that filled my life, so that I might turn to You. You have made me inactive and unable to work, in order that I may become still and quiet. So often I have not listened to Your voice. Now in this quiet I shall listen to You and hear what You say to me.

Let me be attentive when You show me where I have lacked love for You, the times when I have not sought You in prayer, when my work, my family, and other earthly things—passing things—were my idols, which I loved. Make me painfully aware of how little I honoured You, how I scorned Your love and brought You pain. I thank You for the sure knowledge that because You were waiting for my love, You led me into this suffering. Lord Jesus, You are using this illness to knock on the door of my heart and find entrance.

Take my heart. This time You have not knocked in vain. From now on I give You my time. You shall come first, before my work and before the one who has been dearest to me. You shall be first in my life from now onwards. I sincerely intend to obey the first commandment: To love God above all things, because You, Lord Jesus, have loved me so much. For me You went to Your death.   Amen.

*   *   *

*If your illness keeps you from all work and activity,
then the time has come for God to work in you and
create new things. When you are unable to work, God is
able to work great things in you. Also, if you completely
accept the suffering, He will do great things through
you later.*

O Man, each illness will teach you that your life is measured here on earth. Perhaps it will only be a short time before you must face death.

You complain: I must leave life so soon, I have hardly tasted the joys of life; they are so sweet, and now all is ended—for eternity.

You are wrong, Man, in your lament. There is something much more lamentable, the hard fate which awaits you when your soul leaves the earth. God, your Creator, lives. You must stand before your Lord, when your life is ended. He will ask you whether you have loved Him, whether you have given Him your time, your possessions, your riches. He will ask whether you have done what He has commanded in His Word and in the Ten Commandments.

All is not ended when death comes. It is then that your real life will begin, either in the kingdom of joy and great happiness, or in the dread kingdom of tears and lamentation. Those who did not weep over their sins during this life will enter the kingdom of tears. Those who loved earthly pleasure more than God, will go there also.

Come, walk towards real life now. Jesus is the Way. He is the life of your soul. Turn from your old life and live as a new man, whether you are going to live or soon die. Truly you will be full of joy because you will have discovered the purpose of life. You, the created one, will be bound to the Creator. Your soul will find rest in Jesus Christ.

This life is not the true life. That is why God disciplines and chastens us at this time. Sickness and suffering prepare us for a life of joy in eternity,

where there will be no more pain or grief.

A prayer for times when we fear death

My Lord and God,

You know the frightening question in my heart: Perhaps this illness will soon lead to death, when I must leave my life, my work and my dear ones. What happens then? Where shall I be for eternity?

My God, You see that my heart is full of questions, full of pain. I am afraid, Lord, of falling into Your hands—You, the holy and great Judge. You know all I have ever done and have written it all down in a book. You will judge each one according to his works and can cast us into hell.

I cry out to You, Lord, be merciful to me and let me enter Your kingdom of peace and happiness. I bring You all my sins, all that I have done amiss. I will confess all that I can see has been wrong in me. Forgive me. Cover my sins with Your blood, Jesus. You have carried my sins to the cross and so You will rip to shreds the record of my guilt, which accuses me.

I will hide in Your redemption, Jesus. I will conceal myself in Your mercy. Lord, carry me through the dark valley of the shadow of death and bring me home to the Father. I believe in You and lie in Your arms.

I trust in Your might, my Father, and in Your love. You have redeemed me with the precious blood of Your Son. You call me Your child. I am resting in in You. Amen.

My Soul Wants to Go Home

Open, O heavens, wide,

That to my father's side

My soul may wing her way!

My heart's alread-y soared

Above, where dwells my Lord.

O to be wholly with Him!

That day at length will come
All sorrow overcome,
No more will trouble fret
My soul so rapt with joy
Which nothing can destroy,
Nor human mind fully know.

✝

O what rejoicing then,
When trumpets sound again
In triumph and endless joy!
All sorrows then depart,
And joy fills all my heart.
My soul, how blest you will be!

✝

This illness will never come to an end

A letter written to a spiritual daughter during her long illness.

My dear, sick daughter,

What a disappointment the result of your examination was, once again. We can see no end to this illness. I know how this must affect you, what grief it must cause you. It must seem as though your thread of patience will break. Yet it will not break, because it is attached to our Lord Jesus. He was always patient, and He will give you the gift of patience, from His own heart.

Yes, the Lord Jesus never gives us anything but good things, even if it seems otherwise. Such a long serious illness really doesn't seem to be good, but I believe that both you and I have much for which we can praise Him. We know that it has brought good to you and also to me, for I experience and suffer everything with you.

I will make a list of these things for you:

First of all—because your illness has been so serious and carried you to the brink of death, it has brought you much benefit. You recognized several sins of which you would not otherwise have been conscious. But do you remember? Their forgiveness brought you such great joy that in spite of your illness, you could lie in bed all aglow, repeatedly exclaiming, "Never before have I been so happy!"

Then you were taken to the hospital and your illness became more difficult for you. You had to be dependent upon the help of others, even for the smallest things. And this humbled you and it helped my child to lose a bit of her pride and self-importance. It made you a bit more humble and thankful for all the help, love and care of the nurses and doctors.

At this time you were isolated and were able to have practically no visitors. You had to be satisfied with Jesus alone. You spoke much more with Him, because you could not speak with other people. You told me that you came closer, much closer to Him, and into a much more intimate relationship of love with Him.

Now there has been this long period when your patience has been tested, because your condition is not improving. Although you did not succeed in suffering in patience at the beginning, through God's repeated disappointments you have learned to say "Yes, Father", and to pray, "Your will is best". Do you remember that I told you this should be your answer, if the result of this examination should prove disappointing?

So the Father in His love has given you much through your illness. You learned to say "Yes, Father", and learned humility and patience, my dear daughter. Has the Father not given you good things through this illness? He has made you rich—rich in forgiveness, rich in the fruits of righteousness, rich in His love, rich in the happy hours of conversation with Him. You were poor before this illness—but you will leave it richly blessed. It has brought you many of the spiritual blessings for which you have prayed for years.

These only come to us along ways of chastening, and you have been permitted to travel along that road. Soon, very soon, your trial will come to an end. When? Probably, when the Father has achieved the purpose for which He gave you this illness. Then you will be released from this "school of suffering"—but what joy, my dear daughter, when you pass your "examination". Then there will be rejoicing—this is happiness. You will receive new rights, because new roads and new opportunities lie ahead of those who pass their test.

So rejoice over these last miles of your illness—because only good will come to you. Would the Lord God, our heavenly Father, send anything but good things to His child? Believe me, He cannot, because He is the Father and He loves you dearly. So every day that you still have to suffer this illness and home-sickness, repeat, "Only good things come from the Father, only good things." Then everything will become easy to bear.

I am with you in love and join you in saying to the Father, even though we are disappointed because of this last examination—"Only good things come from the Father." Therefore, "Father, we thank You!"

With love,
Mother Basilea

*   *   *

Those who in grief are weeping
Will one day joy be reaping
Beside the throne of Christ the Lamb.
On paths of pain and suffering
Great blessings God is offering
Which multiply in heaven above.

I'll not fear pain or sadness,
'Twill bring me heavenly gladness
And glory at Your wondrous throne.
My time on earth is fleeting,
But there You will be greeting
All those who have a harvest sown.